skeeter bit & still drunk

poems by

Travis Stephens

Finishing Line Press
Georgetown, Kentucky

skeeter bit & still drunk

Publisher: Leah Huete de Maines
Editor: Christen Kincaid
Cover Art: Joan Zoloth - www.zolothstephenswrites.com
Author Photo: Joan Zoloth - www.zolothstephenswrites.com
Cover Design: Elizabeth Maines McCleavy

Order online: www.finishinglinepress.com
            also available on amazon.com

Author inquiries and mail orders:
Finishing Line Press
P. O. Box 1626
Georgetown, Kentucky 40324
U. S. A.

Table of Contents

for Joan

SKEETER BIT & STILL DRUNK

The year was lost. The whole thing buried with a pitchfork,
first twist a lank of grass,
then a stab of dirt. Roots. Keep going.
More dirt, sour & salty,
then the gray rime of clay & gravel.
Make it bigger.
Then kick the year into it.
The dark night of remorse, false dawn promises,
all those soul numbing hours of waiting.

It didn't take long.
Amy looked at the heap of worry in the sour hole.
Might be a clump of rags.
The furry smear found on a roadside.

Nothing to say.
She kicked & worried the dirt
then lay the fork flat to tamp it down.
Stood there & let her heart slow.
A buzz of insects. Something at her ear.

To the south across the fields
a lone car slowed for the turn,
gunned out of it.
Its metal carapace flashed in &
out of the roadside brush.
Engine grew loud, insistent.
Amy stood very still.
Crescendo & tire song.
Nobody comes out this way.
You feed a burn barrel,
keep the rest. Plant potatoes
by the dark of the moon.
She stared at the rough ground
& let the car sound pass,
then fade away.

CHILDHOOD, PART THREE

Rigid lines of demarcation
separated the nine-year-old boys
from the girls.
Boys who were whip
fast on the snowy field, playing
a lawless scrum where the
ball was chased endlessly, until a
boy, just before tackled,
threw the ball to someone else.
Endless scrums and
pools of meltwater—frozen
pants cuffs thawing
under classroom chairs.
Girls stood in the shadow of the
building and formed
allegiances which
were broken by the hour.
Practice, practice.
In a few years,
when boys have finally noticed
girls, they will approach them with a
bit of bravado, a nervous hope.
Of course the girls crushed them.
Stepped on their hearts,
little bugs.

TRAFFIC REPORT

today on the highway
a shattered pile of
wood pieces, jagged sharps
amid a tangle of
fabric and batting.
I believe it was a couch.
A sofa.
Splattered, shattered and tossed.
Stuffing had become cover
& cover had become threads.

Yesterday
on the freeway
between exits
traffic slowed but didn't stop
even as a white van
nosed into the guardrail
facing traffic, poor thing,
billowed smoky flame.
Rain fell as the firemen
lit off the hydrant.

Morning traffic abandons
dogma & prayer for
the solid laws of physics.
The favorite: a body in motion,
second best, equal reactions.
Each day a reaffirmation,
and too often a lament.
Why oh why me?
Why today?

From the right
a flatbed truck merges
bearing a tarp covered load.
I slow to follow.
The tarp is loose

in one corner, a black
shroud of secrecy.
What could it be?
It could be anything:
an articulated clamshell bucket,
emergency generator,
sculpture
for the civic center,
a wrecked Bugatti.
Swaying, rocking.
Ohio plates, is that a clue?
Maybe Lebron's trophy collection
or the relocated mausoleum
of the Bessemer family.
Brake lights.
I go left and let it go,
in my rear view mirror an
ill-shaped lump of commerce.
Maybe headed your way.
My exit seven minutes away.

AMY IN THE CANYON

Amy speaks in riddles.
Amy won't tell you her name.
She lived in a house in the canyon
where artists drank French
wines, then traced recent petroglyphs
onto sheets of Japancsc silk.
Sold them as kimonos in New York, DC,
everywhere good taste is
synonymous with expensive,
 proudly unnecessary.
Amy likes her marijuana, likes
the way it makes rain feel.
She will light a candle, she will
ladle water over stones to hear their
thankful giggles. She says the way
birds tip their eyes to God when
they trickle water is like smoke
into the hollows where a heart used to be.
Amy thinks coyotes are meant
to keep the canyon free of rats, of cats,
and tiny dogs; the dogs which
cannot sleep and decide no one else may.
Amy has many questions.
A coyote yip is a two-tone answer.
She appreciates the way rain
goes downhill, goes into the
best hiding places and then one day
is gone.

LEAVING TULSA

A milkweed city
on the low plain.
A sneeze held in.
Look, no one says Tulsa
without adding Oklahoma
as if there were other
Tulsas out there, as seen from
the Space Station. Look, there's a Tulsa
there's another one. Tulsa, Argentina.
Tulsa, New South Wales. Tulsa, France.
The best thing about rear view mirrors
is that things can grow smaller still.
The worst thing is to lose your contact lens
when the wind lifts it from your finger.
Drive blind. I have a pulse in my tongue
that may be the third cup of coffee
or may be the taste of pin cherry
snatched from the shoulder of the
last road out of Tulsa,
Oklahoma.

COUNTING BEARS

Spring shadow bear in the thick mosquito
house of alder, chewing skunk cabbage
because it is the first green thing she's found.
Sailor bear rolling along the beach, pausing
at a boulder, hunker hug it—Crossfit bear—
lift & roll it to get the mussels and shells
underneath crackling crunching chewing,
the sound of nightmare bear.
Rednecked red-eyed linebacker bear not
liking you, college boy, what you got to say?
Ursus arctos, cousin, americanus, Bro.

That famed island of bears where one man
lived alone, chased bears from his cache of
freeze-dried peas, whole wheat berries. He said
they chose cans of anchovy paste first.
Decades later some kid tried the island
& got eaten.
Blame video games.
Blame the education system.
Don't blame the bears.
White bear of guilt.
Brown bear.
Black in his mortuary suit.
Panda cute & inscrutable.
Once there were gigantic Ice Age bears,
up to 3600 pounds,
who eventually ate themselves smaller.

I fished in Alaska, & rarely saw bears
where there are so many;
exceeded only by Pennsylvania &
New Jersey or the tidy streets of Berne.
Bear flag.
Bear meadow.
Bear bait.
Gone bears. Bear market.

Some of us are becoming bears.
Bear of the underpass,
burrowed into leaves, sage & litter.
Bear of the LA River. Barrio bear.
Bear in the back alley, Venice bear, working
at the new pizza place,
belly bear glad to knead the dough
to lick tomato paste, anchovy off a blade.
Bear asleep in the last shady part of
Dodger Stadium. Bear cups & dogs plus
those packets of unsalted peanuts.
Home run.
Happy bear.
Lumber around the bases.
I am the cousin, hairy & rank,
come to visit too often, stay too long.
Bad bear, the last bear of misunderstanding.

BREAD AND BUTTER

I get my mixes metaphored.
Blame it on books. In third
grade my teacher, Mrs. Butterbrodt,
incorrectly told us that her last name
meant "bread and butter", and
 that her first name meant
"hungry".

She let me choose whatever
 I wished from the grown-up
section of the library.
I traveled by ink.
Darwin. Roy Chapman Andrews
racing across the Gobi
in search of dinosaur eggs. Mongolia
sounded a bit like Wisconsin in winter.
I had not been anywhere; everything
was like Wisconsin. World War I.
Squirrels and bears in hibernation.
Wounded Knee. Munich.
 "Black Like Me" and one book
about a young woman who had been
kidnapped and buried alive.
 She was buried in her nightgown.
Was she cold? Buried how deep?
I didn't care yet if she was pretty, only
if she would be cold. Hungry for
more than bread and butter.

ANOTHER TRAGIC POETRY DISASTER

Reports today of a poetry spill on the 5.
Highway Patrol has all lanes blocked, a real
mess in both directions. It was a truck
which somehow left the highway to fly
nearly over the railings to the open fields.
They are treating it as a possible
terrorist incident. This was highly refined
poetry. PhD quality stuff.

We've all become used to poetry. As I drive the
girls to school we pass tankers of it, warehouses and
 that big MFA factory. It's all part of the literary industrial complex.
The nine-year-old, fatalistic, points at hurried,
unmarked vans. "That one. It could be carrying sonnets."
"No, Elizabeth. Don't scare your little sister."

At the spill, even before the cleanup crews,
there are protesters. One stands before the
camera in a Cowboys jersey.
"It's poison," she says. "No one even knows
how much poetry is too much. How many
parts per million. They give you a little when
you're in grade school and next thing you
know you've got shelves of the stuff."
Reporter: "What should be done?"
"Ban it."
Reporter: "But there has always been poetry. It's
mentioned in the Bible."
 "Then control it. Keep it in silos somewhere like Minnesota
or North Dakota where there are no people."

To become certified a HAZ-LIT response team
must take 16 hours of training with an annual refresher.
First you must learn to correctly identify poetry.

Some of it is easy. Haiku. Villanelle. You learn
to look for indicators: iambic pentameter, trochee.
It is the free verse that gives people the most trouble.
It comes in many permutations. It adapts.
Mutates. I have read that scientist have found
poetry in everything we eat. In the soil.
Scraps of paper blown through fences. In
the sweet flesh of Montana trout.
Traces remain in stoppered amphoras
beneath the Aegean. Bits of poetry
in everything we say.

AMY'S TRUCK

Amy doesn't like clothing stores,
racks of color,
rear mirror glances,
the acid burn from
a lover who said
"you walk like a cowboy".
Once she owned a VW
she named Slash.
Diesel rattle so she
took a class & rebuilt it.
It replaced her only motorcycle,
a Kawasaki 550 left
dead on the road to Madison.
Sold the leather jacket.
Kept the engineer boots
with the thick heel,
the strap attitude.

When she bought her first
car her father came along,
fingered the seat covers,
nodded at the engine oil
stains & radiator full of moths.
He was a botanist &
didn't know a damned thing.
Since then she only
buys from other women.
Amy knows that her pickup
is not a truck, yet she
will help you move
for beer & pizza &
someone else to unload it.
When the same lover
got around to cleaning the garage
the gun cabinet was unlocked,
a pistol missing.
Because Amy had never

expressed interest he blamed
his nephew
that little shit.
Brass is warm in a pocket.
For several months she
mouthed names for the truck
seeing which fit a draft
in the cab, wide seat,
big bones, balky fan.
Alberta, Alberta
where you been so long?

Alberta, the truck, has
a tiny plastic rhino
glued to the hood. It is
faded but fierce, advance
scout for the figures glued
to the dash: raven as lookout,
diplodocus for patience,
mastodon for company. Amy
is seeking a replacement
top for the stick shift—8 ball
or eagle's head. There are
secrets in the glove box.
That gas can in the back is
the start of something
or the fiery end.

BUKOWSKI

we used to joke about drinking
we used to joke about being drunk
drunk with love
drunk with purpose
drink
drank
drunk.
I read that Bukowski is
the poet whose work is
most often stolen.
       Literally.
Taken from bookstores &
libraries in furtive pockets
by like spirits,
alcohol fueled scribblers &
decriers, lovers &
murmurs passing out again.
I should be surprised, but am not.
His was a life of ugly men
moved to write
       beautifully.
Sometimes, he did too.
When I drink
I find a pen moves easier.
Other times not at all.
       Ink is alcohol & dissolved solids.
When the daylight comes
see
what has evaporated &
see what remains.

BISON AT SEA

The foredeck is too hot to touch,
 the only shade on this ketch
found under the mainsail.
We are easing toward Mexico &
California is still to port.

From offshore the live oaks
dotting the sunburnt meadows
look like a herd of buffalo.
I am uncertain that bison
ever shook the ground here.
Did they come over the last
chain of mountains, butt aside
the salt grass, the verbena &
saltbush to sniff at the sea?
Great black noses, what is that,
what is that noise? Did they
think the drum of waves was
another herd, another rush of
cows and calves?

I like to think that a squadron of them
stepped out into the waves, tasted the sea
& chose to go in. Go on. To raise horns,
nose to the light while seals keep pace.
Imagine the stories the fish could tell.

But the bison, buffalo, if they
trod the beaches then surely their
bones lie somewhere in the black
depths of lost history, somewhere
between giant sloth & the uncle
of Ishii. Gone, gone forever.

Closer now, I see the headland is
grazed to domestication. Shadows
of vultures & hawk sweep.
The only mammals left standing are
coyotes, cows & voles.
Sometimes kids on
illegal motorbikes set the grass on fire.
The wind is falling.
Luff and fall away.
We point the boat's nose
into the breeze for a sniff
before turning tail.

ONE LESS

Because Tuesday
lacks the gravity
     of Monday
to arrive late
     on Tuesday
is not a crime.
Today the fog
held the vines
close at hand,
the face of the Bay
     veiled
     mysterious.
Enough to pause
the interminable
commute, pull over
and side road.
     Birds.
An unnamed brook
masking traffic,
the noise of
industry
commerce
and profit.
Who can calculate
the cost of
     one less worker?
In the maw of
the world's
eighth economy
the public radio
recommends a series
of programs.
The brook listens &
murmurs assent.
     I am late, boss,
but not sorry.
Have we learned yet

to monetize leisure
that doesn't smell
      of plastic,
      gasoline
or regret?

FRUIT FLY

I am beset by fruit flies.
I see one and know there are more.
Tiny, furtive speckles of matter,
these may have come from a
sun-warmed dumpster or a banana
peel left out for comic effect.
I shouldn't laugh.
Once I edited a paper on the genetic
permutations of carefully tracked
families—eye pigment, wing shape and
hair color. In the lab they could get
a new hatch in nine days, grandparents
in three weeks. They gassed them with
a squirt of carbon dioxide.
She likely chose me to edit
the paper because I was the only English
degree she knew. Plus I was smitten by
the grey of her eyes and worked for free.

The fruit fly is *Drosophila melanogaster,*
a name that should have been used for
something more interesting, or dangerous,
like a white rhino or Sonoran whipsnake.
Perhaps an armored dinosaur.
Drosophilia melanogaster could be the name
of a recently deposed dictator of a nation
you have never visited.
A comic-book villain.
Today an unchecked, unstudied
swarm of *melongasters* has found me.
One sips from my fizzy glass of Coke
and I hope it drowns.

CARAVELS

We have begun to trace the flight
of my ancestors, trying to lay claim
to the 1492 diaspora, and with it,
EU Passports for all. My son,
fair, as his Anglo father,
coaxes stories from his grandfather.
He hopes to practice law in Madrid
or the Hague. My father recalls
his mother saying that they came
from Russia, originally further west
and travelled through Turkey.
I look at him. We could never
be Ashkenazi; and I was welcomed
throughout South America as
someone returning home. In a
San Francisco restaurant the waiter
addresses me in Spanish. "Do you
know," my daughter, astonished, "how
certain he must be?" She is shiny as
a nickel, another Gentile dad. Then,
"Hola, Maria," she teases, "Quesadilla por favor.."

My newest husband holds his tongue,
bides his time, moody as the sea,
he reads history late at night.
"Imagine," he said, "if Columbus had borrowed
from the Jews to pay for ships, what claim
on a new world." Instead, necklaces,
a reluctant king's kiss.
We did not sail in caravels
followed by birds
or in barkentines recognized by
the heavens.
We came in fetid iron tanks
where the molasses
made the rats fat and bold, their scaly
tails the color of a papist's tongue.

Typhus, TB were some of our new
names at Ellis Island.
Lithuania? You are a painter of buggies?
Cities named Cleveland, Detroit, Tenement.
They did not let us babysit or keep the books.
Not be firemen or cops.
A relative went west and bade us.
Uncle Joe's name is blessed,
my name a version of it.
Garment district, housepainter, pharmacist.
I was born in Los Angeles, as was my mother.
Walk home and light candles that
burn in memory, lighting the faces
of my father, my past, my son.

WRECK ON 29

At seventy miles an hour
eyes open, windows closed,
he drove with one finger
stuck in the wheel, curled
round the rim and knuckles
on the bar. He drove all night.
There is an elegance
to the moon, he reflected,
as its ghostly orb filled
the windshield. I don't
even need my lights.

CHILDHOOD, PART FIVE

Everyone has a childhood, she said.
Some can taste the empty air
in a closet of a house let go.
Some can hear the faraway racket
of laughter at recess
when the mud puddles shrink
and the girls learn a new song.
        What I know is that the days
 began with "Get up, it's chore time."
We climbed from narrow beds
we dressed, cold feet
we stumbled and shrugged
coats, boots, a cap.
        We went to the barn
we fed the cattle
milked the cows
until a dash to the house for
scrambled eggs gone cold,
toast, milk.
Yellow bus might wait if one
of us is at the roadside
wait,
        wait for my brothers.

Wait. You remember the way
the bus stank of gasoline,
bubblegum and too many of us
fresh from the barn.
Woodchucks
the fuckin' town kids called us
but never to our faces.
Anger is the red-faced
cousin of Hate and he, too,
        is my brother.

AMY IN THE PARK

Amy takes her lunch in the park;
she is careful where she sits.
Sun warmed bench or concrete
fountain, depends. Sometimes
she sees children out of school,
the tight knots of girls, elbows,
knees sharp as glass. Boys,
pebbles and gravel, tumbling.
Other times Amy will sit
amid the strollers, listen to soft
voices debate the notion of
a city too clean, leading to asthma,
allergies to circumstance. Peanuts.
Amy thinks of dirt. The miasma
of childhood, clothes on a line.
Toys already loved to pieces when
she got them in brave ceremony.
How much is too much,
how much is never enough.
Today there is not enough mayo
in her chicken salad, too much
celery. Next time, cashews.
Grapes. Unpeeled apple chunks,
raw and dangerous. And salt.
Amy has a vaccination scar
she covers without thinking. She
has been thinking about Native Americans
and how when others—Chinese, Europeans,
Vikings, whoever—crashed their stinking
wooden boats ashore, they sailed
for glory, wealth and for spices to
make their food eatable. Alas,
they found a continent in the way.
Met distant cousins
with a hundred strange tongues
who lived in waterlogged rainforests,
and in arctic deserts.

A plague on them, the sailors murmured,
for not giving us gold, or even a pig.
A chicken. A cow.
Amy might have Native blood, a little,
a twenty-third or less. She has read
that scientists theorize that the
Europeans, crowded, unclean,
have antibodies in their blood from
sharing sickness with livestock.
Born in a manger, perhaps.
Pass it on. Easier to carry than a flag,
a cross or crescent moon. Amy thinks,
sometimes fondly, of her lover.
His humid warmth on cold nights,
yeasty laugh and business-like embrace.
Usually good sex, so a small prick
of conscience; she left him.
Split the blanket. What remains,
she hopes, is a phagocyte, hungry.
A secret immunity in her blood
protecting her from another
handsome, unforeseen stranger
like him.

THIS CONSPIRACY OF RAVENS

My brother the Trickster
washes his sleek, black feathers
in the pool, splashing and ducking
while we watch. We follow him
to the pool and find delicious guts
of salmon, egg sacs, eyes.

There are still a few fish
stranded, the tide has retreated back
to its lair. Last night the bears came.
Fish parts everywhere plus a heaping
steaming grassy pile of bear shit and
packed circles of grass.

This morning we left our home fir,
the five of us, circling like leaves.
In the morning we own the sky.

My brother the Trickster has seen the moon
and where she hides. He has taken the
taste of salt from the rain, has left it
stinking of clouds.
My Brother watches from a branch.
He is making a new song. It has the
growl of an engine, the sobbing of the
drowned, the crackle of a fire. We
laugh and sing along.

BY THE CHIPPEWA RIVER

The end of the bottle,
the end of the evening,
the start to a serious decline.
We are cousins, sort of,
used to standing around,
quiet, beer bottles in hand,
staring into a fire burn, watch
a river sweep by taking stick,
leaves, the rest of the day.

Damn that water looks cold.

Kids dig worms out of
the grass & nobody wants
to make dinner.

This a remembrance
because the body got planted
in faraway Texas & yet
everybody wants to honor
the one who got away.

The men wear T-shirts &
gimme caps, the women in
summer dresses. I am
overdressed in khakis,
upwind from cigarettes.

Remember when he....
damn, that was crazy.
But not as crazy as side-swiping
a concrete pillar at 70
miles an hour, sparks & smoke &
a Chevy pickup shorn of two wheels.
His daughter said they found
his pistol inside the truck but he
was thrown, saying "thrown" the

Texas way with extra syllables.

This is the sour mash,
this is the decanted bile.
Vees of geese circle back
as if north were up for debate.

He played Tevye in "Fiddler",
ironic, given his early flight
into the Air Force. A wife,
another. Nieces who never
met him sniffle in empathy.
His brothers recall a lively tongue,
rabbit punches, his eyes blue
like the river, blue in the sun
yet brown, tea brown &
colder underneath.

A few miles upstream the
Flambeau departs its wooded
cave to join the Chippewa
on its way to town. Last century
the spring log run knotted at
Holcombe, took the bridge,
took seven lives. A great- great-
grandson wrapped his truck
around a Texas bridge pillar.
This river has seen it all,
still sings in the rapids,
still heading south every day.

AIRPORT CUPS

On the morning flight to San Francisco
they hand out little boxes which contain
fruit, a puck of muffin and a tiny plastic
cup of peanut butter. I like to believe
it is some machine squirting peanut butter
into eight hundred and thirty-two cups
not some unfortunate wearing polyethylene
gloves which don't fit well, scooping out
of a number ten can.
What I recall of food service
was loud music, slippery
floors and the way oven doors leave
burns on your wrists; a misery
to anyone who works in hot, soapy water.

There is a dab of peanut butter on the
lip of my box plus a grape stem among the fruit;
 I suspect there is no machine involved.
Likely someone like me,
          brown, restless, dependable.
Facing the endless open mouths of cups,
anticipating, far too much
 the change from peanut butter
to ranch dressing.

WALTER BLANK 1950-2004

Silver strands of barbed wire
lead the blind man in.
The woods is dark, he says,
the woods is my sea of sorrow.
Near the house a swaybacked
collie adjusts an ear. She has fifteen
years of patrol on her record
plus five litters of wooly pups.
Even the crows know her name.

An oil drum, supine and halved,
contains water & a few tadpoles,
its bottom slick as snot. The blind man
kneels to cup water into his face.
The cattle, seven in number, stone footed,
do not mind. They have grazed the
pasture to where only bursts of
bull thistle remain. Pretty purple flowers.
A goat, a sheep, the blind man asks.

The edge of the silo
open to the sky
echoes with pigeons murmuring
prayers. Onto this day let us fly
onto this day let us strut among
the blessed and the worthy.
The barn clutches the silo in its fist.

Because this is Thursday the house is empty,
gone to town.
Because this is September the haircut fields
waver in rain that flees by the day.
Crickets.
When the man finds the dog she lets him
search her coat for meaning, dry his hands.
They walk together toward the road.
Shoulder chokecherries and bramble.

A small oak fleeing the rest.

They asked if he'd like to stay & he nodded,
felt Grandpa's hand on his shoulder, the low
rumble of his voice, the way warm milk
sounds when poured in a can.
Sit on the broad fender
of the first tractor.
Whole days without a word.

Sometimes an aunt visits, cousins, his mother &
the brothers & sister he didn't know.
He's good, Grandpa to his father,
the little man a big help.
It never occurred to him he was meant to overhear.
It never occurred to him that
his parents would move to California.
Walk the path behind the cows,
they like to have their heads rubbed
they like to mock charge the dog,
stand still for the milking machine.
Snow is loud underfoot.
Rain the song of laughter.

To surprise them he will bring
the cows to the barn early, to start
the washing & the milking.
Let them find him in the barn
to switch on the lights & see
the cattle startle at
another day brought to light.

COLD DEAD FISH

Another argument.
I swear
when this night has ended
I will finally leave this place.
I will go to live
in a van parked by the park,
to watch gulls fight
over French fries as I weave
elaborate dream-catchers
of chicken down and wire.
I will push a cart of ice
calling COLD DEAD FISH
to the condos and coffee shops.
I don't expect anyone to buy.
I will learn to play a
one stringed instrument.
I will drink tea made
from yesterday's forgotten crop.
I will stay there
until the broken bones of
my heart re-knit
into a useful pattern.

SHOTGUN AMY

Amy keeps it in her bedroom closet.
Slide one door, a dresser of shirts, jeans, socks.
Slide the other, shoes below hangers & among
them a 12 gauge shotgun.
Like an umbrella, ready in reach. She hangs
a bag of cedar shavings for moths, tries
to pair sneakers, boots two by two.
Amy doesn't like her name.
Tried Amelia, Elizabeth, Beth.
Lizzie the ax murderer, Beth the mouse.
Wishes she had the simplicity of men—
Bob, John, Jim. Not fussy Alexander
or Michael. Nick. She considered a
change to the "A", soft instead of hard.
Ah-my. Like Ah-my brat or US Army, retired.
She mouthed a new name: Shotgun.
It has a finality, a solid bite of purpose.

One of her boyfriends had guns,
kept a box of rifles & shotguns set
near inside the bedroom door.
It saw everything & from the bed
Amy saw the gun safe loom as a
slightly disappointed presence. Aunt Gunny.
Battleship gray. Prissy.
A few times he had opened the safe
to run a hand over the polished
wood of her leg, the walnut stock
smooth as a razor. Touch the cool
barrel & tiny, sensitive trigger.
He hefted one out,
lay it across his lap. Shotgun,
he explained as though to a child.
Twelve gauge double-barrel.
It opened its jaws. Grinned.
Two eyes, black & unflinching.
Got two triggers, he said, but

you set them both off it will
put you on your ass.
He plucked out a fussy rifle,
its slippery bolt, eyepiece. Bullets
shiny as a pawned wedding ring.
He had her hold its dense cuddle,
raise it to her shoulder, cup the barrel.
He was a confident man
who kept a toolbox in his truck,
locked the chrome wrenches away.
Seven sizes of Phillips screwdriver.
A hacksaw, rubber mallet. Monkey wrench.
In the gun safe
a separate shelf for handguns.
"Not pistols. Handguns."
 Holsters of ballistic nylon,
jewel boxes of 9mm, .357 winking back.
His gun safe key lived in a clutch with truck key, house key.
All work keys a separate jangly fist
tossed into a truck cup holder.
Shotgun, Amy mouthed to the silent
witness of her easel. Boom boom.

At the gun shop Amy set her driver's
license on the glass counter like a winning hand.
Tossed her chin to the mirrored cases.
"That pump," she said to Darryl or Roger or Steve.
He unfolded his arms, let the T-shirt
carry the belly over. She saw some fading
on the stocks, nicks and scars.
Mossberg? he said.
"Twelve gauge," Amy answered. It had
a deer foot grip, a pump slide ribbed
for purpose or for pleasure.
Seen some use, said Darryl or Roger or Steve.
Nice model 37. Can toss in a soft case.
Amy saw a string tag dangling from the
trigger. Like in a dress shop.
"I'll take it," she said. "today." Her glance

to a shelf wall of ammunition. Red boxes,
yellow, green. Big fonts. X. Magnum Power.
"Box of six shot," she growled. "One of four."
Each shell thicker than her thumb,
its nail a brass collar cinched to plastic.
Once, as a freshman, she was in the toilet
when an older girl lit a cigarette, snuck
a drag from near the sinks. You look
at a boy's thumbs, she announced to others,
It's how you can tell.
Amy frozen at the pot, face burning at a drop.
All these years later & still
didn't know what that girl meant.

From the closet, the shotgun mute,
the shells lined up red, green
like the worst Christmas decorations.
She put one in her fist
thought brass knuckles
thought Double Oh Buck.
Amy ratcheted the pump again
that lovely clank-clatter of Death
opening the door. She thumbed
in shells, sliding each one in—
four shot, four shot, six, six.
Left the chamber open to touch
a finger to its mouth, firing pin.
Then Amy deliberately
tickled one more four-shot in.
Tasted it on her tongue: Shotgun.

COYOTE IN THE VINEYARD

Crossing the road from one
vineyard to another
the coyote did not pause;
it simply trotted through.
It is early June and the rabbits
too big to catch, the birds
escaping nest each day.
What drives the coyote,
from a dusty set of rows
to enter another? Not grapes,
surely, not yet if at all.
Listen, this is not important.
Why reason or wonder
with a creature so elegant in movement?
A tall fox, a lean wolf set loose.
Afoot, not adrift. Seen and
then unseen once more.

NAMES O NAMES

I have thought some names don't fit and could use revision; other words
are ill suited and as disappointing as your first anchovy.
Why hippopotamus? That should be a flower.
Who would ever eat an artichoke and not risk a Heimlich?
Why not order, instead, a steaming bowl of Mesopotamia?
Plutonium for two, a pot of lamb, fresh crop of harlequin.
Look around at names ill-suited: cute little hand grenade.
That bird? Rapier on the wing.
A flock of filibusters all in a row.
Bulbs for the rare euphonious infantile, planted in the spring.
Jigging for snoqualmie.
A brace of baptist hen.
Nice crop of harquebus among the rodent trees.
Hope for a return to Seaborgium, in the spring.
Other words are adequate and more:
a tank is best left alone; beware the Kalashnikov.
Suffer from pterodactyl or bad Sagittarius.
I lay awake with the dread of metastatic calculus.
Worse of all the I am afflicted with parting,
disenfranchisement and separation. Pale, unfit
words for you, lover, now
Gone.

A SALTY KISS

Along the beach road
gulls keen and argue
above the muted grumble
of traffic.
Cars move steadily enough
that their passing is like
waves that caress the beach.
The sand wanders during storms,
the driftwood,
carcasses of birds & seals,
bone & feathers,
mats of seaweed all come &
sometimes, go.
California is
a long place
with a short memory.
The Pacific is not
made of tears nor
does it sound like
heartbreak.
It glistens in sunlight,
tastes like a lover's kiss,
& whispers
sit here by my side.

WITH THE HERD

I was with the herd today as they
opened the Highway 405 Connector.
Trucks have lined up nose to tail and
they are eager, having waited so long.
At the lead, a matriarch swaying,
rumbling, her flanks bruised and scarred,
paint faded from a dozen winters.
Close behind, the playful pickups and
an awkward panel truck half the size
of the adults. An impatient Mack, cut
off by the youngster, blasts indignation.
Ear-like mudflaps flare in warning.
Soon the entire line is in motion,
a sound of thunder, the earth shakes.
The air is filled with the fresh scent of tar,
exhaust, dust and diesel.
Flanking them, always, nimble packs
of motorcycles take their chances.
It is the circle of traffic, this new road,
made to circle around the city. Before
the Interstate, generations ago, ancient
trucks rolled down gravel roads.
They left a few bony frames in faraway fields.
A hundred risks await—bad fuel, blown tires,
black ice and always, the dreaded collision.
Not today. The herd rumbles on.
Get out of their way.

ABIGAIL

My grade school best friend used
to call me Abigail.
No reason. She just said
I look like an Abigail.
Once I told Rob this. "What to hell for?
You want me to call you Abigail?"
No.
"Jesus, Sue, the stuff you say."

Once I saw a tanned woman in
Los Angeles who wore a tight
gray dress on a Saturday afternoon.
The age of my mother, she
walked a small white dog and her
hair was piled high and topped
with a bun. This was ten years
ago, the trip where Rob caught
that fish while I waited in San Pedro.

We have a son who has
three children by two women,
no wives. The women visit,
leave with ears of sweet corn,
a little cash.
There is a breeze that comes
each day, stirring the clackity
windmill into motion. Sometimes it
smells of salt from far away.
I've seen pigeons ride the wind
like seed thrown to a field. Their
wingbeats say Abigail.

ANYWAY

Disheartened
by reports
of careless plastic
bits in all the waters,
we poke the chair legs
into the wet-dry border &
raise an umbrella.
Before us the buff sand
hot on top, cool below.
My beer bottle displaces
flecks of ivory
that could be anything—
mussel, crab coat,
shrimp armor cast aside.
The sun slaps a wave
& the wave comes ashore.
The flash of silver
in the sand might be
metal, Coke bottle.
But this is the western sea,
the one that trades East
so it might be sake bottle,
bits of bento box threaded
with illegal gillnets. Hardhat.
All tasting of salt, distance
and permanence.
The kid doesn't care;
she raises a city of wet sand,
bucket towers, cup condos.
She dashes for wet sand,
shrieks at a wave's caress.
A perfect day in an imperfect world.

BY A STREAM YOU COULD
LEAP ACROSS, EASILY

From the speckled pond
beneath the streetlamps,
        flit tiny fish.
They venture out to
the ripples, the ruffles,
the downhill run.
They could be trout
or some other
tiny torpedo made of
dancing sinews,
        fins like smoke.
They wear
blue black overcoats
and silver vests,
watchful for the birds,
        the trees,
        pH changes,
        the grasses
littered in sunlight.
Another drain of
a place zoned
semi industrial.
There is no end
to the stream,
trickle additions,
only a growing
water's plunge.
Somewhere
an ocean beckons.

AMY DRIVES FAST

At fifteen Amy had a crush on a ranger
at Glacier National Park. Freckles
across a sunburnt nose. Her family
arrived in late June, the sedan a
nest of books, clothes, fishing gear,
teenage worry and hiking boots.
The ranger was to brief camping parties
on the back country. Three families
gathered in the log center, benches
made for giants, cold stone fireplaces.
Poison oak and rockslides. Racoons.
Hypothermia and snow in the passes.
How to hang a bear canister. Ticks.
The ranger held up drawings that could
have been done by ten year-olds. She
wore a brass name tag that read Brown.
Amy's father told her repeatedly that
the way to remember someone's name
was to use it three times when speaking
with them. Amy watched her father raise
a bold hand, stop the ranger from a
riff on blueberries versus huckle.
"Ranger Brown, do we need a fishing license?"
"Pamela," she answered. "No, it is a National
Park. No license needed." The ranger held
up a drawing of a thick deer. Elk. Her
wide belt had pine cones embossed in it.
The letters USNPS. Strong.
"Pamela Brown, are all the trails open?"
"As of last week, yes. Some upper lakes
are still iced over." Someone wearing Disney
oohed. Amy knew enough about ice.
Didn't need any more snow. She saw that
Pamela Brown had just a lick of downy
mustache, a racoon mask tan of sunglasses.
Take care where you bed down at night.
Some meadow trails are bear trails and

you might be putting your sleeping bag
on their highway. Boil your water. Amy's
mother was gathering fliers, extra maps.
Porcupines are not dangerous. Where her
hair emerged from her hat the ranger had
streaks of light, split ends. Amy chewed
on a ponytail in sympathy. She tanned
well and fast to where the hair on her
arms became invisible, hair white. Last
night her father had her practice fly
casting with him in the parking lot,
swinging the rod up and back, up and
back, ten to two. Lofting lazy waves
of line into the long twilight, a magic
trick of pause and motion. Her shoulder
was sore today, the new bra strap chafing
new flesh. Pamela Brown wrinkled her nose
when Amy's father said her name. Smiled
at Amy, a tiny wink.

Three days later they were
eating trout fried on a campfire.
Amy was practiced at setting up
her own tent, a nylon sculpture of
turquoise. She left the rain fly off
so that the night stars were visible.
Her father had joked about rain flies,
coaxing smiles at horse flies, fire flies,
rain flies, what next? trout flies. Chevy
flies, faculty flies and ice cream flies.
One night she heard her parents make love.
Her mother checked, daily, her supply
of Kool menthols. Sunburn like a blush.

Years later Amy would be driving across
Kansas and Nebraska, her pickup an
easy pal, when a local station played
that Tom T. Hall song done by somebody else.
"I'm the guy who didn't marry

pretty Pamela Brown," the song went,
"educated, well intentioned, good girl
in our town. I wonder where I'd be today
if she had loved me too.."
Amy turned it up loud. Fields gone blond
with late summer, the freckles of
houses and towns beneath a wide sky.
She was crossing the country for a
new job in a town she didn't know.
Her thermos was still half full.
By the third chorus she sang along,
"I guess I owe it all to Pamela Brown..."

ROMANS IN MIDWESTERN AMERICA

I am walking over the prairie as the sun flashes
through clouds, throwing patches of sun and shadow,
giving the impression of something gained, then lost.
It has been a wet spring and plows are late in the fields.
Wind, ever present out here, rakes across these desolate spaces.
Soybean stubble is still on the ground
snapping underfoot but where chaff is not
only bare soil outlasts last year's herbicides.
Stones peer out like bones left to hurried graves.
Piles of huge fieldstones dot the land like the wreckage of war.
Silos rise in the distance, castle towers.
Where roads run like a Roman rule, seeking horizon,
this could be another ancient Hellas.
The dirt blowing from my footprints is my Carthage
still recovering from the salt.

DEATH OF THE OLDS 88

Rust is nothing.
I lost my wheel walls and
all the tinny sheet steel behind
my front tires without missing a mile.
Road salt just makes the time go faster.
Oil pools are hereditary.
I got mine from my first owner;
old gasket gone bad,
overhaul overdue.
They say the wheels go first.
Like Mantle, or Gail Sayers,
my tires are not dependable.
This battery? My third.
I sit beneath this cypress like winter,
like summer gone wild in the grass.
Chigger bait.
Razor grass tickles my radiator.
Mice neck in the back seat.
But I can wait here, fading in color,
and not miss a thing.
The end or the beginning
comes with either a tow truck
or a bucket of gas.
You choose.
C'mon.
Let's take a ride.

GEESE IN FIELDS

There is little mystery
in the dark cold of late
December.
Even in California
cold rises from the earth.
Three days of rain have
encamped for the mountains.
There is a hope
of sunshine tomorrow,
longer days ahead
                and patience,
always patience.
Geese have landed
in pools within fields
to snap at left grain like
misers set loose in a vault.
Vees of others pass over,
exchange insults or pleasantries
or both while a footsore
young coyote measures
the growing shore.
This is an artificial lake;
it will not last through summer.
Her hunger, though, is real.
The errant breeze regales
her with the scent of geese,
tadpole and distance between.

Sky breaks open,
a cloud grazes, ambles on...
In the pasture of sky
from Sonoma Mountain
to the headlands
a roundup has begun.
No branding irons needed
no horses to ride

just watch
the cloud hands gather
tally, corral grey mares.

They mill,
flick tails in annoyance.
Restless, dangerous
contained.

All is on pause,
the rain falling
and more to come.
Roots break from the
mud to catch a breath.
An egret stands at the edge,
patient, poking
into the blanket silence
so easily broken.

KAPLAN GYM

Saturday
at the pickup game
movement is horizontal.
Some outside shots,
squeaky shoes & the hollow
punk of dribble.
Isolation ball.
Nobody sets a
pick and the matchups are mostly equal.
Tall nervous gunner
versus the point guard.
Heavy versus bad back.
Surviving middle age is mostly
just showing up.

Half court is enough.
This gym has low rafters;
long shots haven't a chance.
With the big doors propped open
the sound of children is like birds.
Jack wears a jersey over a T-shirt.
City Champions, 1983.
His head fake fools no one.
Sometimes a sparrow darts in,
rises to flutter at the skylights.
It will find its way out; always does.
No one watches the game
unless they want in.
Sure.
Come around next weekend.

THIS BLOOD SOUP

Virus
is just another way of saying
I am with you. We share
the salt of tears, the copper
and iron of our being. This
will never go away.
Without meaning to, I have
made antibodies and cells
to match yours, to absorb your
entreaties and make us one.

We live behind closed doors.
Blame the strangers.
Because they lived with cattle,
because they dined on sheep and bristly pigs,
they had resistance. They came.

Our people lay in the embrace of
the only land they knew.
A few survived, scarred and scared;
even their language withered, tasted
of copper and the dust of weeping.

The strangers live among us now, numerous.
Plant a flag, cast the seed.
Let them be killed
by bacon or heart disease,
violence or another self-inflicted error
whatever
lurks in the dirt of their past.
The stranger
that new tiny one
number Nineteen.

AMY DOESN'T DANCE

Amy doesn't trust her feet.
The hull beneath her might be a lawn,
overgrown with hidden stones, thistles.
Clump, bump ankle itches.
Once, she must've been ten or twelve,
her mother, snappish before coffee,
said, "you could be a horse on the stairs".
Amy never forgot it.
Some women move to music and
with it; a tango, a waltz. She wonders
what livestock hear. Bovine. Porcine.
Animals like her with clumps of wood
at the end of legs, not dancing but
made to drum along.
For the past few months Amy
has been dating a dancer, who
she met in physical therapy;
her dislocated shoulder,
his dislocated knee. Wet floors, both.
His upright carriage an inspiration,
his shaved body a surprise. He loved
her dirty laugh, her one pot meals
that bordered on disaster. Amy, he said
short for America. He is Argentine,
more polo than gaucho. Even
on crutches he pirouettes.
Bored, afraid of losing his place,
she drove him to ballet rehearsal.
There he spoke breathy Spanish
to a chain smoking mannequin.
Amy stood near the barre
as the dancers leapt in sweats.
She learned that, up close,
ballet shoes are bullets and that
some ballerinas grunt, some
sweat a lot, will swear and
whose tiny, airborne feet
sound like hail and thunder.

WHY THE FISHERMAN FEARS DROWNING

Beneath its busy surface, the waves, the chop,
foam and frother, the ocean has deep pockets of calm.
Where whale booms and the click of dolphins
are a whisper across a vast room.
If you drown at sea, you won't go there.
Likely you would be set upon early in your descent,
while the sharp torpedoes and gnashers can see you.
Some would tug & some would nibble
& some would find a way into the pod of you, to slip into
mouth or anus and take up residence. Until the ribs are
a cathedral and the bony egg of your thoughts is licked
clean. Then the eels may depart, or accidentally knock
out a wall, leaving the now unworried husk behind. To
drift, to diminish and eventually sink.
To where the light is gone.
Down here are the Mesolithic horrors,
 the unlit valley of fear and crazy.
Things with teeth. Things with little lures & a mouth
bigger than the body. Worms. Eyeless wriggles &
slow moving bitey things which subsist on a shower of
faeces, dander & detritus plus an occasional mangled bit.
The pressures here would turn you into a bit of jelly,
studded with bits of bone, like the worst fruitcake imaginable.
There is no reason to get in the water, man.
Nobody knows that better than me.

NIBBLE

Where the Pacific Coast Highway has
six lanes north of FREEWAY ENDS
cars slow, jostle, worry. I've got
my windows down, coasting to
play with the MPG numbers.
To my right, proud on a bit
of shoulder is a young rabbit.

What?
Three feet from rabbit is this
span of cars, left of that expensive
homes then expansive sand.
Past that the salty edge of the world.
Beach bunnies.
To the right that rise of cliff
to Santa Monica. ROCKSLIDE AREA.
Dirt thatched with mustard, yucca & coyote brush.

The rabbit nibbles unworried.
Cool kitten. A cony island.
High above there is a park where
people like to sit & watch the sea,
like to throw bottles & shopping
carts & bicycles in a jangle hop.
How many rabbits are hiding?
In the cruel mathematics of nature
how many sisters &brothers
to this stalwart , were lost in the
litter, the gravel & open skies?
Bury the past.
A group of rabbits can be
a warren, down, trace.
I am in a river of cars, also
known as a jam, commute
or everyday disaster. If there
were a shoulder beyond
this sharp toothed curb

I'd like to pull over. Sit
in the dirt & chew a stem of grass.
Buck wild & not
move a thing.

THE ACE HOTEL

has become apartments
voices and laughter
in another room

mail pile by the door.
a spring clip to collect
rent checks plus a
marker message in
three-inch letters:
DON'T LET ANYONE IN.

a pay phone
perhaps the last pay phone
in Seattle.
today I answered it:
"Jim?"
"almost. John"
"Put Jim on."
"I don't know any Jim."
"Everyone knows Jim."
"is this a wrong number?
how about number seven?
I like seven
or nine and a half."

"that's how long we were
married, just couldn't
make that second digit
speaking of which, there is
one she left me

middle one, you guessed it
ha ha, pretty funny now
but not at the time"

"You sound like Jim."

DYLAN BLUES

Tom Waits is being piped in,
saying "Hold on."
I cannot seem to get enough
caffeine into my blood,
these torpid
middle of October blues.
Listen, they gave Dylan a Nobel.
Anything is possible.

I can't help but think of Jay Bob Scott
from Neponset, Illinois.
 Jay.
 Bob.
 Scott.
Man of three first names,
who was my relief on the tour boat.
He didn't know anything
about diesels, sure,
but everybody liked Jay.
So for three days a month
he was enough.
I think of Jay
because he would leave
notes for me about the
engines,
generators,
props,
steering,
anything that
might cause a problem.
His notes always ended with a Dylan quote.
Don't think twice, it's alright.
I left notes in kind;
pumps and vandals,
got to serve somebody,
joker man.
It seemed as

though Dylan had lines
for anything, if you kept
it loose enough.

Later I fished with
Ten Knot Tommy
who found a "Wizard of Oz"
song for every fishing day—
Courage.
Home.
If I Only Had a Brain.

So in October of another sideways
year I wonder
if either Dorothy or Dylan
have an answer for the blues.
Ask the woman waiting in line,
wearing coveralls, as I know them,
boiler suit or jumpsuit. Hers
is form fitting, snug where she
would want it to be, generous to
a fault. Onesie, twosie.
Do coveralls honestly work
with a push-up bra?
Nearby, a man in a fedora.
Not trying too hard at all.

I watch a pot-bellied man of about my age
climb onto a bike for a ride.
He's leaving Starbucks,
pedaling to wherever
his wife will lead.
She has a camera mounted to
her helmet,
a lean hungry look.

Ask the rumpled writer
scratching away in his journal.
All of us dipped in indigo.

What I am trying to say, man, is
maybe the best advice of
the day is simply
Hold On.

BIRDS IN ALTERNATE PLUMAGE

The reporter says the fall fashions
run to big shoulders and slouchy boots.
Plum and magenta makeup trends.
Men go for logos and random lettering.
We are waiting for a table at NOBU, pushed aside
by the predatory singles.
Have another sidecar, Bub. That line won't work on anyone.
We come for the strong cocktails, the
lobster tacos, but mostly for the people watching.
A scene, Eileen. A show, Jo.
Such as the girls clustered near the bathroom
who must have giraffes in their bloodlines
yet not enough material on hand for a decent skirt.
Don't look twice, it's alright.
I say girls, for they are not old enough to drink;
but old enough to have someone buy them one.

Look, a woman in full drama. A man in fedora.
Who does that? A grown woman in a onesie.
Coveralls and pumps, a pushup bra struggling to
impress a thousand-dollar pair of jeans.
That hoodie? Famous for the wrong reasons.
Beyond the deck sand pipers dash along
retreating waves dressed in semi-formal
gray evening wear. If given chance would birds
dress up? Sweaters of kingfisher blue, a cloak
of cardinal or the royal sweep of peacock?
I imagine parrots complain about the price of
housing while trying on a magpie tail,
that short black raven dress.
Asking, is this too much?
While standing outside the surf,
dour egrets look down their long beaks,
do not approve, still waiting for a table.

ONE HAND CLAPPING

I woke with a palm pressed to my face
chin cupped, fingers splayed
over lips, over nose & cheeks.
My palm.
The hand smelled of sleep after
a Negroni, of bad teeth &
time to get your ass up.
Maybe the dog woke me.
Or a dream of my father's hand;
wide fingered & nicotine,
a farmer's hands looking for something to do.
Somehow I inherited an affliction
where my little left finger has quit work.
It curls up like a sleeping puppy
ready to lead a fist or to
seek the pillow of my palm.
It has a name, this affliction, which
is a tightening of finger cords.
It is a gift from Northern Europeans,
mostly, sometimes called Viking finger.
Nose picker. Snot scratcher.
I woke reminded that I am a mutt of
poorly made pieces, not tall, not short,
not worth looking at twice. My kind
show up in newspapers in disaster sites—
carwrecks, barn fires, another business failing.
Among the handful of onlookers at
the scene of the crime.
We used to be so numerous
we used to make a softball team.
Finger the ball, let Grandpa play.
This bed is as far from my childhood as possible.
Hand in hand walking the beach.
For the flight west & almost success,
give the guy a hand.

PONY GIRL

Around the vast cedar tree
 the girl is circling.
A pony, she says, I'm on a pony.
Three steps behind, the feral boy
says no, you're not, but his forever
clogged nose, snotty nose, made him
sound as if he were underwater.
He is suffering from the early
onset symptoms of first love.
My pony can prance, she says,
and skips in flashes of patent leather.
This is May, almost June. Snow
has gone back to where it comes from
and in a few weeks he will never
see her again.

Later his therapist would encourage him
to use memory as "a springboard to emotion",
as if his emotions were very far away.

In truth his hard face and blue
eyes made him seem distant, like
a blackjack dealer or sometimes
killer. Emotions were the rage
and despair he tried to bury,
the mystery that intrigued new
lovers yet left them uneasy.
There were good reasons not to
keep a gun in the house, reasons
why he had a large family that
lived far away. In memory's
darkened rooms a young girl is
circling a tree, prancing, while a
boy, hopeful still, tries to keep up.

BITES

We are comprised of bites—
some welcome, some not.
Bites & what is left surrounding
the bite. Welts. Scabs & sores.
Appleseed ticks, grossly swollen
grapes of black blood, mosquitoes
so many goddamn mosquitoes
& their cousins, the gnats, the midges.
No good idea goes unpunished.
No good comes out of stagnant pools
criss-crossed by waterskaters &
dragonfly squadrons out for a good time.
Mysterious bite marks
along my waistband
ankle burns
new & gone.
Midday moon like a balloon
of love, veiled in possibility
yet with one contemptuous eye
for rockets & rovers &
other lunar assaults.
On the dark side no one
can see all its bites &
scratches.

FROM AFIELD

My kingdom is the edge of the field,
 the narrow groove
of the dead furrow.
All grass is above me.
All sky is staring
at my mid-mouse nose
twitching, finding
        dust
        a thistle bite
        dirt like bile.
From the dead furrow
the creaking corn
is laughing
leering at the shadow
growing larger.
Hide in the rows
        if you dare.
They will tell the crows;
they will invite the fox.
From the dead furrow
the night looks familiar
if not safe.
        Firefly
        star
        a moon's lazy smile.
When the dew comes late
I drink.
Another day.
Victory.

COUNTY ROAD D

Flying
the car had left the road,
leapt from the asphalt
into the brush & grass of
a roadside leading to marsh.
She left the road at a rate of
speed only estimated at,
uncertain,
yet the course was straight
off the road,
out into the night.
The car left a path of broken grass,
& shattered weeds,
 a great swath of anger.
She flew off the road &
through the Grace of God
into the marsh.
She walked away.
She walked away after
she woke up, wondering,
where am I
why is there water all around me.
Walked out &
found the car dead,
the key on, still in gear.
Did the car die of water
or of sudden stop?
This teenage driver
should have been dead,
should have hit a tree.
Six miles of wooded road &
her path the only clear one.
She walked out,
out of God's hands & into
the morning
still drunk.
Muddy angels

held her trembling hand
& held back those of her father,
disbelief & anger,
fists & kicks
overwhelmed
by relief.
My baby girl.
My God.

RAIN ON SUNDAY

Rain has come
lingers
too comfortable by far,
the weekend guest
no one really wanted.
Frogs hallelujah
rising creeks,
growing ponds,
drowning mice.
On this day
the sky is stooping
close to the trees
burying is runny nose
in the branches.
Rain is talking
in the quiet voice
of a Sunday morning.
Rain all day.

THEY KNOW WHAT TO DO WITH THE MURDERED

They know what to do with the murdered.
When found,
        & I hope all are found eventually,
the murdered are given study,
an intense scrutiny exceeding that of a lover.
Every hair,
every inch of the body.
The pose, the surroundings,
time of day are considered, recorded.
Photos taken.
There is a process.

Shine an ultraviolet light, ask the questions.
Samples of dust, of clothing taken.
Murder weapon.
Science wades in even before a
coroner's formal assessment.
Case number, lead and team assigned.
Television & movies document how an
investigation is done.
Cue the dramatic music.
They know what to do with the murdered.

No one knows what to do
with the family of the murdered.
Talk ceases.
Looks away.
At first maybe an interview by police,
a formality,
like their condolences.
Maybe a quick question & nothing more.
Maybe a television camera,
often not.
Custody of the beloved will wait, must wait.
Someone else makes brutal incisions,
more samples,
broken skull,

ligatures after hours.
Take a break.
Slow, careful stitches which no one should ever see,
a thread of story interview.
The clock is ticking.
Is there a witness?
          Of course there is,
but beside the murderer
who else saw this,
who broke the skull,
          who broke the story?
Can I get a witness?
Hard chairs.
Choked back sobs,
brief, uncomfortable phone calls.
Not many answers.
They know what to with the murdered
but not with the hole
where my brother used to be.

16th OF SEPTEMBER

September has reached the zenith,
passed the mid-point of completion.
End of summer
end of the growing heat
the end of long days.
In the vineyard they sample
the fruit for sugar and juice.
I imagine a taste of cabernet,
a riddle of chardonnay.
Unnoticed, jackrabbits scatter, quail
dash and vultures soar.
What has lived thus far
will likely continue to.
This is the end to the
brutal extravagance of
random victims;
of numerous hatchlings,
schools of fry,
and helpless young.
From here the winter is
taking hold, testing its grip.

END

ACKNOWLEDGMENTS

The author's gratitude goes to the editors of the following journals, in which the poems in this book, sometimes in earlier versions, first appeared:

2River: "This Conspiracy of Ravens" and "Traffic Report"

American Journal of Poetry: "Bukowski"

Cathexis Northwest Press: "anyway"

Crosswinds Poetry Journal: "Leaving Tulsa" and "Why the Fisherman Fears Drowning"

The Dead Mule School of Southern Literature: "Ace Hotel" and "Death of the Olds 88"

The Finger: "fruit fly"

Gravitas: "Romans in Midwestern America"

GRIFFEL: "bites"

Gyroscope Review: "Counting Bears"

Havik: "A Salty Kiss"

Hole In The Head Review: "By the Chippewa River"

Ink & Voices: "Airport Cups" and "Pony Girl,"

Kissing Dynamite: "name o names"

Miletus Magazine: "County Road D"

Night Picnic Journal: "Bread and Butter" and "With the Herd"

Offcourse: "Amy Doesn't Dance" and "Dylan Blues"

Open: Journal of Arts and Letters: "16th of September" and "one less"

Otis Nebula: "Bison At Sea"

pacificREVIEW: "Childhood, Part 5"

Peregrin Journal: "Rain on Sunday"

Prime Number: "nibble"

The Ravens Perch: "skeeter bit & still drunk"

Raw Art Review: "Kaplan Gym"

Red Fez: "Abigail" and "birds in alternate plumage"

Red Planet Books: "from afield"

Route 7 Review: "This Blood Soup"

Sheila-Na-Gig: "Geese in Fields," "Amy in the Canyon," "Amy in the Park," and "Amy Drives Fast"

Silver Needle Press: "Wreck on 29"

Speckled Trout Review: "Walter Blank 1951-2004"

SPECTRA poets: "Caravels"

Stoneboat Review: "Coyote in the Vineyard"

Tiny Seed Literary Journal: "By A Stream You Can Jump Across, Easily"

Two Cities Review: "Amy's Truck" and "Shotgun Amy"
Variant Literary Review: "Another Tragic Poetry Disaster"
Vessel: "Amy Doesn't Dance"

My mother first encouraged me to read and my debt to her is renewed every day. Thanks to my storytelling parents and grandparents, plus to my siblings—Bill, Mick, Verne, Theresa and Keith, and my relatives throughout Wisconsin. Thanks to Art and Helen, and to Julia and Jake who have enlightened my life beyond measure. For the professors at UW-Eau Claire—Bruce Taylor, Martha Mihalyi, Roberta Hill Whiteman, and the late Dick Kirkwood—my gratitude endures even after so many years. To my fellow poets far and wide, I applaud you and your voices. Last, to Joan, my love and gratitude unending.

Travis Stephens was raised on a Wisconsin dairy farm. He graduated from the University of Wisconsin-Eau Claire and has worked as a welder, veterinary tech, barrista, commercial fisherman, cook, and handyman among other things. Eventually he became a sea captain and currently manages a tugboat company. He lives in southern California with his family and is striving to make the perfect chocolate chip cookie. His poems and short stories have been published in numerous publications both in the U.S. and abroad. This is his first book.